An adult robin perched in a berry bush

Robins

Jill Kalz

A⁺

Smart Apple Media

COPYRIGHT

Published by Smart Apple Media

1980 Lookout Drive, North Mankato, MN 56003

Designed by Rita Marshall

Printed in the United States of America

Photographs by Brian Gosewisch, KAC Productions (Kathy Adams Clark, Bill Draker, John & Gloria Tveten), George Robbins, Root Resources (Wanda Christl), Tom Stack & Associates (Sharon Gerig, John Gerlach)

Library of Congress Cataloging-in-Publication Data

Kalz, Jill. Robins / by Jill Kalz. p. cm. – (Birds)

Summary: An introduction to robins, describing how they look, what they eat, how they raise their young, where they live, and more.

ISBN 1-58340-131-8

1. Robins–Juvenile literature. [1. Robins.] I. Title.

QL696.P288 K36 2002   598.8'42–dc21   2001049641

First Edition 9 8 7 6 5 4 3 2 1

Robins

CONTENTS

Musical Messengers

How do we know that spring is here? The sun feels a little warmer and shines a little longer. Snow melts, and tulips poke through the soil. Lawns turn green. And the *cheerily-cheer-cheer-cheerily* song of the robin fills the air. For many people in North America, spring unofficially begins when American robins return from their winter homes. These birds fly south each fall to escape the cold, sometimes traveling as far as southern Mexico. In March, as it gets warm to the north, the robins return. Few birds are as common or as welcome in

people's yards as the robin.  American robins are found all across North America. They make their homes in cities and towns, forests, and prairies—just about any place that has trees.

Robins are a common sight in North America

Their cousin, the European robin, lives in woodlands and backyards throughout Europe and western Asia. The two look, sound, and act quite differently, but both belong to the same family of songbirds, called thrushes.

Robin Details

Best known for its reddish-orange breast and cheerful song, the American robin is about 10 inches (25 cm) long. Gray-brown feathers cover its back, and white rings encircle its eyes. Male robins have a darker head than females, but both have a black-and-white throat. Black spots cover young robins'

breasts until they are about five months old. Male

American robins sing, but females do not. Males usually sing

to attract a mate or to mark their territory. Both males and

The colorful feathers of an American robin

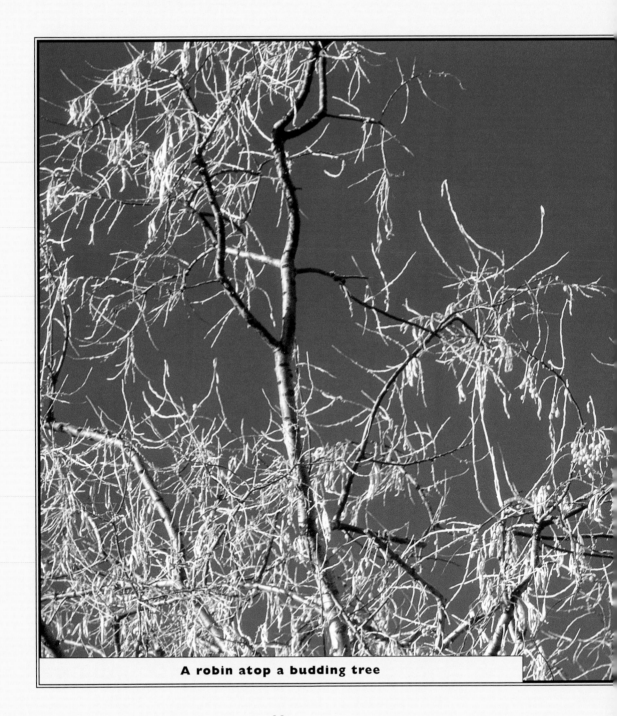

A robin atop a budding tree

females talk to each other using a variety of calls, including a

cheep, a *tuktuk,* and a scolding chirp. Although the

earthworm is one of robins' favorite foods, **invertebrates**

make up less than half of the birds' diet. **A baby robin may eat more than half of its own weight in food each day.**

Robins love fruit. They feed on cherries, grapes, apples, tomatoes, and many different kinds of berries. The robin's straight beak

helps it pluck food easily from the soil or tree branches.

A robin feeding on berries

New Families

In the fall, when temperatures drop below freezing, fruit withers and many insects die. Many American robins must then migrate to warmer climates to find fresh food. They travel in groups called flocks. In the spring, male robins return north first to set up territories.

American robins are strong but slow fliers, usually traveling just 35 miles (56 km) per hour.

When the females arrive a few weeks later, males sing to attract their attention. Once a female robin has chosen a partner, she builds a nest. American robin nests are made of twigs,

grasses, and even bits of string or paper. Mud holds everything

together. The female uses her body to mold the nest into a cup

shape. She then lines the inside with soft grasses. Robins

Robin eggs waiting to hatch

prefer to nest in trees, but their nests can also be found on windowsills or atop barn rafters. The female lays three or four small blue eggs and then **incubates** them. After about 12 days, the eggs hatch.

Newly hatched baby robins, called chicks, are completely helpless. Their eyes are closed. They have no feathers.

Baby robins punch their way out of their shells using a special "egg tooth" that falls out shortly after they hatch.

And they cannot feed themselves. Robin parents may make 100 food trips per day to feed their chicks' huge appetites.

A baby robin calling for food

With good care, however, chicks are ready to leave the nest in just two weeks. Because chicks grow so quickly, parents may have time to raise up to three families in one summer.

The Big World

Young robins just out of their nests are fairly good fliers. But until their wings are stronger, they often just hop around on the ground. During this time, they are easy targets for **predators**. Cats, raccoons, snakes, and large birds such as hawks or owls are the robin's main enemies. And there are other dangers for robins. Cold snaps or snowstorms may

kill hundreds of robins during migration. Robins may be

poisoned by lawn chemicals. They may fly into windows.

Because of these threats, the average life span of a wild

Hawks often hunt robins and other birds

American robin is less than two years. The world can be a tough place for robins, and yet they continue to thrive. They fill the air with their cheerful songs. They help us control pests by eating thousands of insects each day. And they brighten our parks and backyards with their beautiful red-orange color. Spring just would not be the same without its bright-eyed messengers!

The American robin is the official state bird of Connecticut, Michigan, and Wisconsin.

Beetles make good snacks for robins

Worms for Dinner

Worms are one of robins' favorite foods. For this game, pretend you and your friends are robins, and see how many worms you can catch!

What You Need

Construction paper
Scissors
Metal paper clips
A ruler
A piece of string three feet (.9 m) long
Tape
A small magnet

What You Do

1. Cut out 10 squiggly paper worms. Each worm should be about one inch (2.5 cm) wide and four inches (10 cm) long. Attach a paper clip to each worm's head.
2. Tie one end of the string around one end of the ruler and tape it so it does not move. Then tie the magnet to the other end of the string.
3. Scatter the worms on the floor. While kneeling on a chair, use the ruler to "fish" over the backrest. See how many worms you can catch in 10 seconds. The player with the most worms wins!

Earthworms burrowing in the soil

Index

Words to Know

incubates (IN-kew-baits)—keeps eggs warm so the chicks inside will grow

invertebrates (in-VUR-teh-brits)—creatures without a backbone, such as worms, caterpillars, or beetles

migrate (MY-grate)—to move from one area to another according to the changing seasons

predators (PRED-eh-torz)—animals that hunt and eat other animals

territory (TAIR-i-tor-ee)—an area claimed by a male robin as his own; any trespassing males are attacked

Read More

Jenkins, P. Belz. *A Nest Full of Eggs*. New York: HarperCollins, 1995.

Kottke, Jan. *From Egg to Robin*. New York: Children's Press, 2000.

Willis, Nancy Carol. *The Robins in Your Backyard*. N.p.: Birdsong Books, 1998.

Internet Sites

About.com, Inc.: Birding/Wild Birds
http://birding.about.com/hobbies/
birding

Kid Info: Birds
http://www.kidinfo.com/science/
birds.html

eNature.com
http://www.eNature.com/guides/
select_birds.asp